The Home–School Guide

Reading with Young Children

for parents and other helpers

G000145521

Carol Matchett

Contents

Early Learning Goals for the Foundation Stage

Sounds and key words for children in Reception classes

Schofield & Sims

1 Reading together

Why is reading together important?

You have probably been sharing stories, books and rhymes with your child since he or she was born. By doing so, you have already started your child off on the road to becoming a reader.

Sharing books is important for the following reasons.

- Your child learns by watching and listening to you; from your example, he or she will learn what 'good reading' sounds like.
- Listening to stories shows your child that reading is about finding meaning and making sense.
- It will help your child learn how books and stories work.
- Your child will want to learn to read if he or she sees you reading.
- Sharing stories helps to develop your child's language – and that will help him or her learn to read.

When children start to read for themselves, is reading together still important?

Children begin to read for themselves when they start school. They bring books home from school, to practise reading. Some schools send books home for parents and children to share together. Other schools invite parents in, to choose books with their children.

Yes, reading together is still important at this stage. Even if the school doesn't send books home for sharing, it is important to carry on doing it. As a young reader, your child still needs the enjoyment of being read to, so you should continue to make time for sharing a story together.

> **Remember**
>
> Sharing books is fun! It shows your child that reading is fun. Try to make sharing a story together a daily event.

Things to remember when reading with your child

What shall we read?

- Choose stories *with* your child, so that you can share a book that both of you will enjoy.
- Re-read 'old favourites'. Encourage your child to join in, or take over the reading of familiar parts of the story.
- Read information books as well as stories. Young children love stories, but your child is probably now becoming interested in the world – and asking lots of questions! Read information books and enjoy finding out together.

Bringing the book to life

- Be a model reader! Show your child how to read with fluency and lively expression. Use your voice to bring the story to life.
- Talk about the book as you read it (see Section 6, **Talking about stories**, pages 12 and 13).

Opportunities for speaking and listening

- Language is made up of four interdependent strands: speaking, listening, reading and writing. You can use stories as a focal point for speaking and listening activities, as well as for reading.

Brainwave

Ask the child questions about what you have read together. This will encourage your child both to think and to talk. Your discussion will help to develop the child's language as well as his or her understanding of the story.

2 Hearing your child read

What is meant by 'hearing your child read'?

When children start school, they build on early reading experiences and take their first steps in learning to read. Sometime during your child's first year at school, he or she will probably start to bring home a 'reading book' – a book to read aloud to you at home.

Remember, 'hearing your child read' should never be a stressful experience for you or your child! You are still sharing a book together. It should still be fun and enjoyable. The only difference is that your child is the main reader, rather than you.

How can I help when hearing my child read?

When children are learning to read they have a lot to think about. You can help to support your child by giving encouragement and reminding him or her what to do – this book will help you.

Sometimes children bring home a book that is a little too difficult. If your child is struggling with a book, help him or her out. Share the reading so that you read the more difficult parts and your child reads the easier parts.

If your child comes home with a book that seems a little too easy, don't worry! Lots of enjoyment and learning can come from reading something simple.

Remember

Set aside a special time for reading. Choose a time when both you and your child are happy to read. Don't choose a time when either of you are tired, or would rather be doing something else.

Brainwave

Allow your child time to think. A pause does not always mean that your child is stuck – he or she might be thinking or working it out. Wait before you jump in!

Some guidance on hearing your child read

Before you begin reading

- Have a look through the book before you begin your reading session, so you have an idea where your child might need help. Some books (such as the **Daisy Lane Home–School Readers**) include notes and ideas for how you can support your child.
- Sit down together; place the book so both of you can see it.
- Don't go straight into the book 'cold'. Talk about the cover and suggest some ideas about the story: for example, '**I wonder if …**' Make sure that your child is eager to read.

As you read

- Use praise to show your child what he or she is doing right.
- Remember that we all learn by our mistakes. When children are learning to read they will make mistakes. They need to know that this is OK. They need to feel confident. Always praise them for 'having a go'.
- Talk about the story – it will help your child to make sense of what he or she is reading.
- Don't make the session too long. Ten minutes is probably enough. A number of short sessions are always better than one long session. If it's a struggle – stop! Try again some other time.
- Always end on a positive note, with lots of praise.

What next?

- Reading a story more than once can give your child confidence, so return to the story another day and read it again. The repetition will encourage your child to read fluently and with expression. But don't overdo it. There is no point in reading a story again and again if your child is bored with it.

3 Making sense

What's it all about?

Reading is about understanding the words on the page. The process of reading can be a bit like solving a puzzle. There are lots of clues to help you solve the puzzle and discover the sense of the words.

- Some of these clues are 'phonic' clues – they relate to letters and letter sounds (we will look at phonics in Section 4, pages 8 and 9).
- If the book is illustrated, the pictures may provide clues.
- The knowledge that reading must 'make sense' also gives important clues.

Why is 'making sense' important?

When children know that reading must make sense, they have learned two important lessons.

- If something *doesn't* make sense, it probably means that they have made a mistake. So they must stop, go back and look at the text again.
- Sometimes you can 'guess' a word you are not sure of by thinking about what you have already read. This is not really guessing – it is making an 'informed choice'! The picture, the context and the flow of the sentence all help children to choose a word that makes sense.

Remember

If your child gets stuck with a particular word, ask him or her what word would make sense.

Encouraging your child to 'make sense' when reading

Using the pictures

- Talk about the pictures in the book. Draw attention to what is happening in the picture before your child reads the words. This will 'tune in' the child to what the text might say before he or she reads it
- Use the pictures to introduce difficult words such as the names of characters, or unusual objects that you know your child will not recognise.

Taking time

- Don't 'jump in' as soon as your child makes a mistake. See if he or she can work it out alone. Praise your child if he or she stops and realises that something didn't make sense.
- Sometimes, allowing time to 'take a run at the word' can help children guess difficult words in the middle of sentences. Say the rest of the sentence, leaving a gap for the tricky word. Hearing the sense of the sentence will help your child to work out the missing word.

Wrong word, right meaning?

- Sometimes your child will say the wrong word, but get the right meaning. Praise what the child did right – he or she chose a word that made sense – before you draw attention to clues that help work out what the correct word is.

4 Phonics – learning letter sounds

What is phonics?

Words are made up of letters and each letter stands for a different sound. When you know the letter sounds you can build up the words. This is called phonics.

Why is phonics important?

Phonics gives young readers important clues when they are working out what a word is. To use phonics, young readers need to learn the following.

- To listen for sounds in words.
- To recognise which letter shape makes which sound.
- To blend letter sounds together to read words.

How can I help my child learn about phonics?

Books like the **Sound Stories** in the **Daisy Lane Home–School Readers** series use rhyme and word play to focus on the sounds of words and letters: they introduce phonics in a 'fun' way.

- Rhyme helps to focus on words that end with the same sound, but have a different sound at the start of the word.
- Sentences or jingles made up of words beginning with the same letter help to focus on the sound of particular letters.

Brainwave

Go on a letter hunt – at home or when you are out. Look at signs, instructions, packaging; car number plates are great for capitals!

Remember

Teach your child the letter *sounds* before the letter *names*. Teach *lower-case* letters before *capitals*. Introduce letter names and capitals later, as your child gains confidence.

How to play with sounds

- Read rhymes and rhyming stories. Pause before the rhyming word and ask your child to 'guess' it. Make up rhymes based on those you read.
- Make lists of rhyming words by changing the sound at the start of a word ('hat', 'sat', 'mat', 'zat') – some of the words can be made up!
- Read text that features lots of words beginning with the same letter sound, or make up your own 's̲illy s̲ound s̲entences'. Exaggerate the first letters.
- 'I-Spy' helps your child listen for sounds at the *beginning* of words. Later, ask your child to find words that *end* with a given sound.
- Play 'The Tray Game'. Ask your child to put on the tray an object that *begins* with a given sound. When your child can do this, ask for objects that *end* with the sound (*middle* sounds are more difficult!)

Learning about letters

- Show your child a letter shape and say the sound. See how many times he or she can find the same letter on the page or in the book.
- Use magnetic, foam or plastic letters for matching games. Show your child a letter and ask him or her to find another the same. Talk about the shapes of letters ('round', 'tall'). Match capitals with lower-case letters.
- Look at two letter shapes that can be confused: for example, 'n' and 'h'. Ask, 'What is the same?', 'What is different?'
- Write letters using different media (crayon, paint, pencil). Or write a letter in a sand tray, saying the sound as you write. Ask your child to trace over it.

Using phonic knowledge

- Show your child how to build or read three-letter words by saying the letter sounds and blending them. For example, '"p-o-p" makes "pop"'. But saying letter sounds is not always the best clue to reading a word. Sometimes you need the key words approach as described on pages 10 and 11.
- Remind your child that the first letter of a word gives a clue to what the word is. Help him or her to say the first letter sound when reading a sentence with a tricky word. For example, 'Max t____ him a joke.'
- Find two rhyming words in a book ('bug', 'tug'). Talk about the letters that are the same/different. Use plastic or foam letters to make the word 'bug'. Change the first letter to make new words and help your child to read them.

5 Reading common words

Why are common words important for children who are learning to read?

There are some words that we find in every book: for example, 'the', 'and', 'it', 'was'. It is useful for young readers to learn to recognise some of these words and it is comforting for them to see some words that they already know when they pick up a new book.

Some schools will send children home with words to learn 'on sight' – that means that children should learn to recognise those words straightaway, whenever and wherever they see them. Support your child by helping him or her with this learning process.

How can I help my child to recognise common words?

Books with lots of repeated phrases are useful for teaching children to recognise common words like 'in', 'the', 'look'. Books like the **Key Word Stories** in the **Daisy Lane Home–School Readers** series have the same words repeated on a number of pages. This means that there are lots of opportunities for finding a word and looking at it closely.

Remember

The best way to learn words is by looking for them in lots of different places – in books, on posters or signs, in newspaper headlines, on boxes and packaging. Make the best use you can of the rich language environment around you.

Schofield & Sims **The Home–School Guide to Reading with Young Children**

Helping your child to recognise words

Words in books

- Point to a word. Ask your child to find the same word on a different page.
- When reading books with repeating patterns, ask your child to point to the words as they read them. Pointing focuses on reading the words rather than just memorising the text.
- Before reading a new book, ask your child to look through the first few pages and find words that he or she already knows. This can help a nervous child feel more confident about tackling something new.

Looking closely

- Talk about the shape of different words: for example, '**a long word**', '**a short word**'.
- Write words using different media (paint, felt pens, rainbow crayons).
- Make words out of magnetic, foam or plastic letters.
- Use the letters to make two words that are similar, such as '**the**' and '**they**'. Ask your child to say what is the same and what is different. Then ask the child to make '**the**' into '**they**' and '**they**' into '**the**'.

Using words in context

- Use common words to make labels for use in the home: for example, '**My** _____', '**The** _____'.
- Make clues for a treasure hunt using common words like '**Look in the** _____'. You can use pictures for more difficult words that describe hiding places: for example, '**basket**', '**garage**', '**bath**'.

6 Talking about stories

Why is it important to talk about a story?

Whether you are reading to your child or your child is reading to you, it is important to talk about the story.

Talking about the story helps your child to

- focus on the meaning
- make sense of the words on the page
- learn how stories work
- develop language.

And it makes reading fun!

When should we talk about the story?

You can talk about the story *before* you read, *while* you are reading and *after* you have finished the story.

- Before you read, talking helps to build up an eagerness to read and find out what the story is about.
- As you read the story, talking can help your child make sense of what is happening.
- When you have finished reading, talking will help your child to think more about the story and understand it better.

Brainwave

Re-telling a story in your own words is another way of talking about stories. The 'told' version can be very different to the 'print' version. Your child can use the pictures in the book to help retell the story. Or the child could act out the story using toys or puppets or miming the actions.

Remember

Talking encourages thinking. Ask 'why' and 'how' questions as well as 'what' questions, for example: **'Why did ...?'**, **'Why was that a surprise?'**, **'How did ...'** Use some imaginative questions, too, such as: **'What would happen if ...?**

How to talk about stories

Before you begin reading

- Talk about the title of the story and the illustration on the cover. You could introduce who or what the story is about: for example, '**This is a story about a toy hippo. He is very silly …**'
- Pose questions that might be answered by reading the story: for example, '**What do you think …?**', '**I wonder if …**'

As you read

- Ask questions and comment on the events. Encourage your child to do the same. '**That's funny …**', '**I wonder why …**'
- Point out things happening in the pictures that are important to the story.
- Talk about *why* things happen. Make sure your child has understood links between events.
- If you ask a question, give your child time to think before giving an answer.
- Stop at interesting or exciting points in the story and encourage your child to predict what might happen next
- At the end of the story, comment on the events, for example: '**Well, what a surprise!**', '**I liked it when …**' Encourage your child to do the same.

After you have finished reading

- Relate the events to the child's own experiences or to other stories he or she has read. '**This reminds me of …**', '**Do you remember when …**'
- Discuss the events in the story: for example, '**What happened first …?**', '**Then …?**' Make sure your child gets the events in the right order. Look back through the book to check what happened when. Talk about how the events are linked.

Remember

Language is made up of four interdependent strands: speaking, listening, reading and writing. You can use stories as a focal point for speaking and listening activities, as well as for reading.

7   Understanding books and print

When you pick up a book or a newspaper you know how to start reading it and you probably take this knowledge for granted. But for children who are just learning to read it is not always obvious. Which way up should they hold the book? Where should they begin reading?

What do young readers need to know about books and print?

The following are just some of the things that young readers need to know. Perhaps you can think of some more.

- When we read a book, we start at the front and turn the pages until we get to the end.
- In English, we read print from left to right and from the top of the page to the bottom.
- Print is made up of words – and words are made up of letters.
- Between each of the words there is a space – otherwise we wouldn't know where one word ends and another begins!
- Stories are written in sentences. A sentence ends with a full stop. The full stop tells the reader to pause.
- A sentence is not the same as a line. Sometimes a sentence runs onto the next line, sometimes it does not fill the line.

Remember

Your child will learn by watching you handling books and listening to how you read stories.

How to help your child to learn about books and print

Learning about books

- When you are sharing a story, talk about what you are doing – for example, why you pause at a full stop, or how you are going to read the print at the top of the page before that at the bottom.

- Use words like 'cover', 'author', 'front', 'back', 'full stop', 'capital letter'. Children learn these words quickly when they hear other people using them.

Learning about print

- Ask your child to point to the words as he or she reads them. This will demonstrate that your child understands that print is broken up into separate words. It is fine for your child to stop pointing to the words once he or she has become a fluent reader, as pointing can spoil the flow of the reading.

- Check that your child knows where to read next on reaching the end of a line, a section or a page. Show the child if he or she is unsure.

- There are words all around you in your everyday world. Make the best use you can of this rich language environment.

Brainwave

Give lots of praise when your child does something right, for example: **'You remembered to stop at the full stop – well done!'**

Early Learning Goals for the Foundation Stage

The activities described in this book will help your child to work towards the following Early Learning Goals (ELGs) and Stepping Stones.

Language for communication

- Listen with enjoyment and respond to stories, rhymes and poems and make up own stories, rhymes and poems. (*ELG*)
- Extend vocabulary. (*ELG*)
- Use vocabulary and forms of speech that are increasingly influenced by experience of books. (*Stepping Stone*)
- Explore the meaning and sound of new words. (*ELG*)

Language for thinking

- Use language to imagine and recreate roles and experiences. (*ELG*)
- Use talk to organise, sequence and clarify thinking, ideas, feelings and events. (*ELG*)

Linking sounds and letters

- Continue a rhyming string. (*Stepping Stone*)
- Hear and say initial and final sounds in words, and short vowel sounds within words. (*ELG*)
- Link sounds to letters, naming and sounding the letters of the alphabet. (*ELG*)

Reading

- Explore and experiment with sounds, words and texts. (*ELG*)
- Re-tell narratives in the correct sequence, drawing on language patterns of stories. (*ELG*)
- Read a range of familiar and common words and simple sentences independently. (*ELG*)
- Know that print carries meaning and, in English, is read from left to right and top to bottom. (*ELG*)
- Show an understanding of the elements of stories such as main character, sequence of events and openings. (*ELG*)